KNEES
AND GREAT
LEGS

BABBIE DeDERIAN

LONGMEADOW
P R E S S

To Chena, Liz, my intelligent typist, Richard Gallen,
Mom...and most of all to M.B.D., if he hadn't dumped
me, there'd be no KNOCKOUT Knees!!!

Copyright © 1987 by Babbie DeDerian
First Longmeadow Press edition published 1993
Published by Longmeadow Press, 201 High Ridge Road,
Stamford, CT 06904.

Cover design by Kelvin Oden
Interior design by Gregory Thomas and Associates
ISBN: 0-681-41568-1

Library of Congress Cataloging-in-Publication Data
DeDerian, Babbie.
    Knockout knees and great legs / Babbie DeDerian.
        p. cm.
    Originally published under title: Knockout knees and great legs in
30 days: Los Angeles: Price Stern Sloam, © 1987.
    ISBN 0-681-41568-1
    1. Beauty, Personal.   2. Leg—Care and hygiene.   3. Exercise for
women.   I. DeDerian, Babbie.   Knockout knees and great legs in 30
days.   II. Title.
RA778.D32   1992
646.7'5—dc20   92-14440
                                                            CIP

Printed in United States of America
Second Edition
0   9   8   7   6   5   4   3   2   1

When I was interviewed for the first edition of this book four years ago, I knew it would be a great success, as it has been. It is a wonderful guide to self improvement addressing all aspects of beautifying the lower extremities. The good news is that today with the most recent advances in exercise, beauty treatments, and body sculpting, the second edition of this book widens the possibilities for even more women to obtain exciting and gratifying results.

Peter Fodor, M.D.
Plastic Surgeon
President, Lipoplasty Society of North America

Knockout Knees and Great Legs was written and originally published in 1987. It is in print in several languages around the world. The inspiration for its content was the impact the return of the mini had on all of our lives, as well as our previously—covered—knees. When I stood in front of a mirror holding my skirt a few inches above my knees, panic set in...my own legs were not in as great shape as they could or should be. There was no doubt about it, if I wanted to wear the mini the second time around, I would have to raise the standards of my legs before I could raise the length of my skirts.

The mini has since become a classic...*Knockout Knees and Great Legs* will never go out of fashion ...and you can't afford to ignore your legs as you swing through the 90's and into the 21st Century.

You too can make your legs two of your greatest assets if you try.

Table of Contents

introduction

Hemlines may rise and fall as fashion dictates, but it will never be fashionable to lower the standards of our legs.

Great Legs are Here to Stay! They're not just a fashion fad...the latest whim of some designer...or this season's excitement from the runways of Paris or New York.

Legs have become Big Business! The shoe, stocking and sock industries are booming...short skirts have become a classic staple in all of our wardrobes...and women who aren't happy with the legs they were born with are spending millions each year to reshape them with exercise, or restructure them with liposuction. There's no doubt about it, legs have gained a focus all their own. Miracles may not grow on trees...but we can work magic on our limbs!

Back in 1987 when the return of the mini hit the front pages of the *Wall Street Journal,* I set out to get my own knees and legs in shape to bare. For several months I went from exercise class to exercise class...seeking advice from physical fitness experts who taught me a wide variety of toning techniques...I experimented with dozens of beauty products, using them on my legs for the first time...and then I consulted with several board-certified plastic surgeons and dermatologists to get the latest update on surgical procedures to remove abnormal fat deposits and spider veins.

With the help and advice of these doctors, beauty and fitness experts, I developed a simple routine that worked for me...and will work for you. Not only did I succeed in reshaping and strengthening my legs, but I also improved my posture and the elasticity of my skin.

In the process I proved we can all have toned, taut and terrific legs, regardless of our age or weight.

Knockout Knees and Great Legs was written to share the results of my own efforts. Since most of us are already up to our kneecaps in exercise and calorie counting, this book is effortless and yet effective and inspiring. By following the program for the next thirty days, you will streamline your knees, ankles, and calves without the pain or strain of working out, walking or weighing in...and you will be rewarded with the bonus of a tighter butt and thinner thighs. Because it isn't the weight you're carrying, but the shape of those legs that are carrying the weight.

The mini is here to stay...all eyes are on your KNEES, CALVES, and ANKLES.

get to work on your legs today!

You will see appreciable results in seven days and an astounding improvement in less than 30 days

But before we get to work, I promise you won't have to . . .

- Go to the gym or health club
- Set aside time to exercise
- Go on a diet
- Run or swim miles every day

knocking your knees

How to rate the basic shape, tone and texture of your knees, calves and ankles

whether you need to . . .	• Build up or trim down the muscles of your calves • Pare down the fat around your knees or • Streamline your ankles
you can count on these results . . .	• Eliminate knobby or chubby knees • Shape up scrawny or heavy calves • Trim less-than-graceful ankles

To begin, measure your knees, calves and ankles just the way you measure your chest, thighs or hips, making note of the length, width and tone of your leg muscles as well.

Write down your measurements and put them aside — you won't look at them again until your 30 days are up.

Now, stand in front of a mirror (a three-way mirror is best, but a small mirror held up to a full-length mirror will work, too) with your skirt pinned three or more inches above your knees.

Analyze your entire lower leg — knees, calves and ankles — from the front, rear and sides.

rate your calves and ankles	A ☐ Sexy and sensational B ☐ Not bad, but not toned and tight C ☐ Too thin and underdeveloped D ☐ Shapely but too heavy

now rate your knees	A ☐ Round, athletic and firm
	B ☐ Bony and knobby
	C ☐ Knock-kneed
	D ☐ Dimpled and chubby

Give yourself one point for each A) answer, two for each B) answer, four for each C) answer and six for each D) answer.

your score	**Two—**
	Your legs are great already. The 30-day workout will keep them that way!
	Three to seven—
	By the end of the first week, you'll see an improvement.
	Eight to eleven—
	In 30 days, your legs will be great!
	Twelve—
	You may need two or three 30-day sessions, but it's worth the effort.

now analyze your kneecaps	A ☐ Silky-smooth and supple
	B ☐ Wrinkled and dry
	C ☐ Rough and red
	D ☐ Covered with sandpaper

If your answer was "yes" to B, C or D—almost a sure thing if you haven't been pampering your legs the way you already pamper your face — you'll be delighted with the results of Chapter Four's health and beauty routines.

Evaluate and Compare . . .

Other women's KNEES, CALVES and ANKLES.

rate your knees and legs on the scale of 1 to 10	**8-10** Knockout and great	**4-7** In better shape than you thought. And with a little work they can be great	**1-3** In need of much improvement, but worth the effort

Of course you can cop out at this point . . . keeping your skirts long and your KNEES covered. But who would want to? Based on the consensus of all the above you're ready to proceed.

Now that **you've set your goals . . . and analyzed what you have to work with,** it's time to **consider your options** . . . and get to work.

You'll be glad you did **in less than 30 days!**

short skirts
are ready
for your legs

now let's get
your legs ready
for short skirts

knee-and leg-ercises	Quick-toning tips and fourteen leg-shaping exercises to develop, strengthen and trim your knees, calves and ankles in 30 days

You will notice that I'm not telling you to stop your life for 20 or 30 minutes or even an hour to do specific exercises a certain number of times.

That's what's special about this book: the point is for you to fit these do-while-you're-doing-something-else exercises and toning tips into your regular day-to-day life.

All it takes is motivation — and just by buying this book you've already convinced me you're ready to make the minor adjustments it will take to incorporate my exercises into your daily routine.

These exercises and toning tips are designed for you to do at your desk . . . in line at the bank . . . walking up stairs . . . doing the dishes, as many as time and patience allow.

Once you get into the habit of doing these exercises whenever and wherever, chores will seem less tedious . . . time spent waiting or working will pass more quickly . . . and you will give yourself a "pat on the knee" as you see your legs respond and improve without the strain or pain of strenuous movements.

Obviously the more exercises you do, and the more often you do them, the faster the results, but don't worry if your count seems to differ from day to day.

Personally, if I'd had to keep a record of how many knee sways, heel hangs or calf stretches I did every day, I would have gotten bored and lost sight of my goal.

As long as you integrate them into your daily routine, you will have executed an effective and impressive number by the end of each week.

If you haven't been doing any other exercises, on a fairly regular basis, **you may want to continue for a second 30-day cycle. But do not get discouraged.** You will begin to see and be able to measure an appreciable difference in 14 days.

**let's
talk about
standing tall**

When working on any part of your body, good posture is crucial. To see if yours measures up:

- Draw a straight chalk line down the middle of a full-length mirror.

- Stand in front of the line, facing mirror sideways. The line should bisect your earlobe, shoulder, waist and hip joint, fall **behind** kneecap and **in front of** anklebone.

  For good posture, proper spinal alignment is a must. If your spine is out of line, do this to align it:

- Pull lower abdominals in towards lower back.
- Pull up on waist and rib cage, so torso is nice and long.
- Head up, shoulders down and relaxed.

---

breathing tips

Proper use of your breath will increase flexibility during your stretches by relaxing the muscles. They will lengthen through the slow-static holding stretch. Inhaling first through the nose, and then exhaling through the mouth slowly as you press into your stretch, breathe gently as you hold your position.

**health and
toning tips**

- To build up calves, go barefoot at home, walking on the balls of your feet. Better yet — turn on your favorite music and dance around the house on the balls of your feet.

- Always stretch out your lower legs after wearing high heels all day.

- When walking, use the heel-ball-toe step: Put heels down flat, roll forward onto the ball of your foot and then, as you begin to step with the opposite foot, down on your toes.

- Begin all exercises slowly and try to link the end of one exercise to the beginning of the next.

exercise tips

Anti-gravity exercise is best for toning your lower legs. Consider swimming.

- When flexing, keep knees straight and legs fully extended. You should feel a stretch from your foot through the lower leg and up to the upper leg.

- Slow movements build muscles up and fast movements break muscles down, so adjust your pace for the results you want.

- There's no need to exercise strenuously. Overworking your muscles leads to a build-up of lactic acid that causes soreness the next day. Massaging your muscles after exercise can avoid the build-up.

- Our bodies are like rubber. We can increase our flexibility by stretching into a movement rather than forcing it.

KNEES

1. knee squeezes

Do at your desk, putting on make-up, watching television or talking on the phone

1. Sit upright with feet flat on floor, about hip width apart, holding a soft rubber ball between knees.

2. Press knees together, squeezing ball.

3. Release and repeat with even movements.

4. Alternate between even movements and a series of squeeze, hold, release and repeat.

5. This can also be done standing.

Benefits: inner and outer knees

Bonus: inner thighs

2. knee sways/ leg lunges

Do while washing the dishes, vacuuming or brushing teeth

1. Stand straight with feet two feet apart, toes pointing out.

2. Bend right knee over right foot, shifting weight to right leg and straightening left leg, keeping feet on floor.

3. Return body weight to center, keeping knees bent slightly.

4. Bend left leg over left foot, shifting weight to left leg and straightening right leg, keeping feet on floor.

5. Repeat transfer of weight back and forth with even movements.

Benefits: calves and shins

Bonus: thighs

3. knee stretch

Do while watching television or talking on phone

1. Lie on floor, feet stretched out straight.

2. Flexing right foot and bending leg, bring right knee up to chest.

3. Raise flexed leg straight up in air and straighten knee.

4. Point toes, keeping knee straight, and lower leg slowly.

5. Repeat with left leg.

Variation

1. Lie on floor, feet stretched out straight.

2. Flex right foot and lift leg straight up.

3. Point toes, keeping knee straight, and lower leg slowly.

4. Repeat with left leg.

Benefits: entire leg

Bonus: abdominals and buttocks

4. double knee stretch

Do while watching television or talking on the phone

1. Lie on floor and breathe in.

2. Breathe out and bring both knees into chest.

3. Bounce knees back and forth toward chest three times from hip joints.

4. Breathe in and stretch both legs straight up with toes pointed.

4. Flex both feet, breathe out and bring legs down slowly.

5. Relax and repeat.

Benefits: backs of calves

Bonus: inner thighs

5. knee press

Do while talking on the phone or watching television

1. Sit or lie on floor, resting on elbows, knees bent and feet flat on floor.

2. Making sure knees are open wider than hips and feet point outwards, press one knee towards center of chest, gently stretching thigh.

3. Breathe while holding stretch, release, and repeat on other side.

Benefits: calves and outer knees

Bonus: thighs

6. standing knee bends

Do while you wait — in line at the bank, the copy machine or the water cooler — or at home, brushing your teeth or blow-drying your hair

1. Stand with feet apart just wider than hip width, toes turned out slightly.

2. Keeping back straight, chin level and heels on floor, bend knees directly over toes.

3. Lower and raise body with smooth even movements, keeping knees bent at all times.

Caution: bending with feet spread **too** wide can build up muscles on outside of hips

Variation
1. Stand up straight, heels together and toes turned out.

2. Bend knees out over toes, keeping heels on floor.

3. Rise up on balls of feet.

4. Straighten knees and stretch legs, pulling up through legs and backs of knees.

5. Roll down from balls of feet to heels and back to original position.

Benefits: elongates calf muscles, stretches arches, strengthens feet

Bonus: tightens and stretches inner and upper thighs

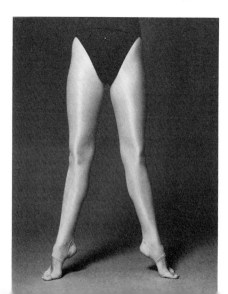

7. calf stretch/ butt and thigh tightener

Do while talking on phone, watching TV

1. Lie on floor, knees bent, feet flat, hip width arms out.

2. Slowly raise butt, pulling in abdominals and squeezing butt, keep upper back and shoulders flat.

3. Roll up heels as high as you can.

4. Hold.

5. Slowly lower back to floor, keeping heels raised.

6. Lower heels. Repeat.

Benefits: Achilles tendon, calf, ankles, knees

Bonuses: front and rear thighs and buttocks

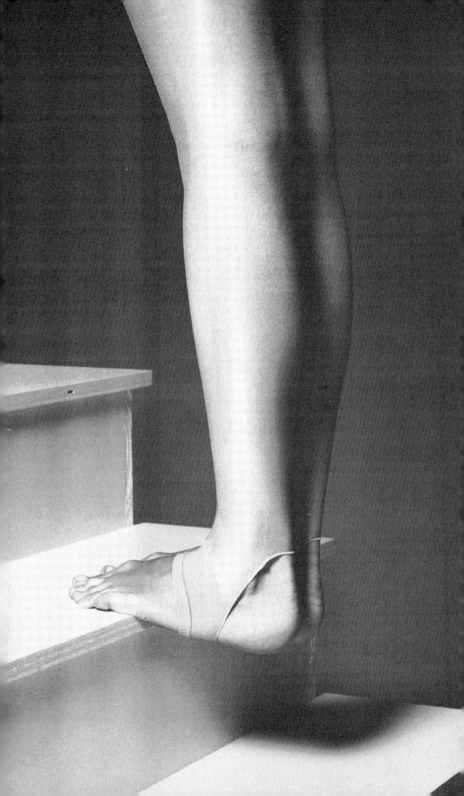

8. heel hang/calf stretch

Do while walking up stairs or on an up escalator

1. Holding onto a handrail to keep steady, stand with balls of feet on step and heels hanging over edge.

2. Gently lower heels. Hold until you feel a stretch through the back of calves and ankles.

3. Raise heels level to step and repeat.

Benefits: stretches tendon, works calves

Bonus: flexibility

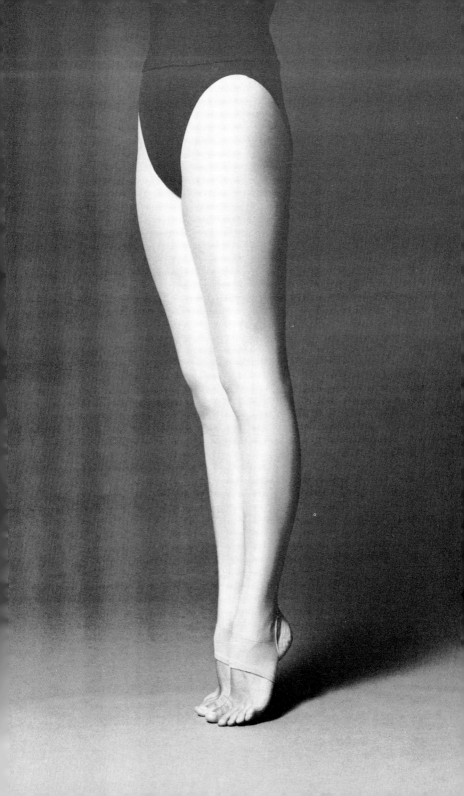

9. standing heel lift/calf stretch

Do in elevators, waiting for a bus or in line at the bank

1. Stand tall, feet close together and toes pointing straight ahead.

2. Steadying yourself on a railing, shopping cart or door knob, lift both heels and press balls of feet into the floor.

3. Staying balanced, gently lower heels back to floor without placing them on floor completely.

4. Raise again.

Benefits: calves and backs of ankles

Bonus: inner thighs

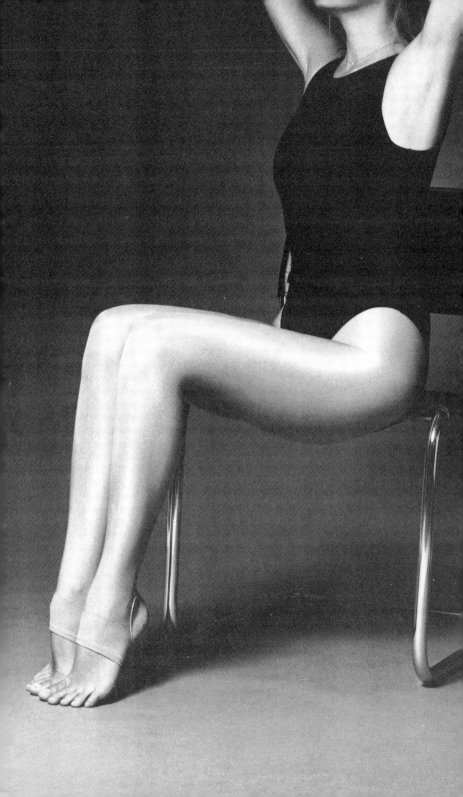

10. sitting heel lift/calf stretch

Do at your desk, in a restaurant or commuting to work

1. Sit up straight, shoes off, feet flat and close together with knees touching.

2. Lift both heels and press balls of feet into floor, squeezing knees together tightly.

3. Gently lower heels back to floor without placing them on floor completely.

4. Repeat, raise, squeeze, lower, relax.

Benefits: calves and backs of ankles

Bonus: inner thighs

11. calf shapers

Do while talking on the phone, reading a book or watching television

1. Sitting in chair with back straight, raise right leg to stretch straight out from the hip.

2. Flex foot, toes perpendicular to ceiling, and then raise straight leg one or two inches.

3. Point and flex a few times.

4. Lower and repeat.

5. Repeat with left leg.

Variation
1. Sitting in chair with back straight, raise right leg to stretch straight out from the hip.

2. Turn inside of outstretched right knee toward ceiling, toes turned out.

3. Raise outstretched leg one or two inches, then lower.
3. Repeat with left leg.

Benefits: stretches calves, works backs of knees, thighs and shins

Bonus: tightens hips

12. super calf stretch

Do in bed or on the floor watching television or talking on phone

1. Lie flat, legs stretched out straight.

2. Raise legs together slowly.

3. Reach up and grab ankles (or as close as you can get).

4. Flex feet, pushing heels towards ceiling.

5. Point toes and hold position until you feel a stretch through your knees and calves.

6. As flexibility increases, try to hold your toes.

7. Release feet and lower legs slowly.

Benefits: stretches calves, works thighs and knees

Bonus: upper arms

13. foot flexes

Do on the floor reading a book or watching television, in the tub or at your desk

1. Sitting up straight, bring feet together.

2. Point toes, flex feet, point, flex, pushing down on toes and then out with heels.

Variation 1
1. Spread legs open wide and repeat above, feel the inner thigh stretch.

Variation 2
1. With legs open, add ankle whirls. Rotate flexed feet, pointing toes as you go down and return to flex.

Benefits: relieves leg fatigue in calves, stretches Achilles tendon, metatarsal arch and tendons

Bonus: inner thighs

14. hip flexes

Do on the floor reading a book or watching television

1. Lie on back, legs straight.

2. Bring right foot across left thigh, opening hip and pressing knee to floor. Use your hand to help press the knee down if you need to.

3. Hold and breathe.

4. Repeat with other leg.

Benefits: calves, inner and outer knees

Bonus: buttocks, inner thigh

**climbing stairs
need not be a
chore**

Many of us moan and groan when we have to climb up stairs on a daily or occasional basis. Consider yourself lucky if you have to and practice the following at home, in the subway or at work. If you don't walk up stairs as part of your daily routine, use the stairs between floors at work instead of the elevator for one or two floors.

As you move from step to step, swing free leg back and out behind before you place it on next step. As you get more comfortable with this exercise go on to raise and tend the free knee before you swing and stretch out. Feel stretch in calf and back of thigh as well as tightening of butt.

It may take you twice as long to get to the top, but you'll be in twice as good shape as you were at the bottom.

**now you can
be inventive.**

**discover your
own variations
and places to
work out!**

leg dressing
Legs have gained a fashion focus
all their own!

Leg dressing and leg wear have become an important part of getting dressed each day. You can dress your legs to accent your clothing, reflect your personality, make a dramatic, coy, or provacative statement or simply color them to match the mood you're in...and to catch the eye of that certain someone you're out to impress.

The return of the shorter skirt is a blessing and all the fashion ammunition a woman needs to make friends with the opposite sex. Statistics and leg-istics have proven...*men prefer women in short skirts*, so don't be bamboozled into lengthening yours in the near future, especially if you've just gotten the courage to uncover your knees. A show of legs in a short skirt is far more fun...takes years off your age...and takes up less room when it's time to pack.

Legs, once restricted to wearing orangy-brown pantyhose, can now step out with new pizzazz. The leg revolution, which began with the emergence of opaque black pantyhose, has since exploded into a wide range of thigh powered leg strategy...and, if you're an adventurous flirt who likes to take colorful chances, there's a huge array of enticing styles and colors you can collect and wear to reinforce your leg positions.

The Do's and Don'ts of Leg Dressing
It may be perfectly leg-al to use your legs to attract attention and steal a man's heart, but it's totally illeg-al and an outright crime to have:
Sagging stockings...if your legs are thinner than you'd like,

build them up with my leg-ercises, but in the meantime wear stockings with a little Lycra. They will contour to their shape and size.

Crooked seams...if your legs are less than straight, and the least bit bowed, stay away from seams altogether.

Runs...especially if you're wearing black or dark colors. It's one of the no no's that turn men off the most. Carry an extra pair in your purse or keep one in your desk.

Busy patterns...if your legs are heavy, stick to dark solid colors, especially black to create the illusion that your legs are thinner than in fact they actually are.

Be playful...daring...and cunning when you dress your legs. You can turn them into pussy cats or tigers, vixens or vamps...sorcerers or scholars.

If you'd like to play the vamp or vixen, but don't know how to get started...garter belts are racy and sexy especially in dyed hot colors. So is a sensational single lacy garter.

If you're out to make a psychedelic neon impression...layer lace tights over fluorescent pantyhose and watch them glow.

If you want to be touched...wear nylon with the look and feel of silk.

If you're short and would like to add the illusion of height...try horizontally striped pantyhose.

If you're young and outrageously flirtatious...start collecting whimsical and whacky socks in mad patterns, stripes and dots to call attention to your ankles.

If your intent is to seduce...indulge in a pair of over the knee thigh-highs which will allow a provocative inch of bare leg to show.

To hide imperfections that may bulge or ripple...matte jersey or opaque satin tights will work wonders.

If you stick to basic clothing...you can make a stronger statement with your legs. Never mix patterned clothes with busily patterned or heavily textured hosiery...the effect will be too confusing and scramble your transmission, undermining the messages you are trying to convey.

For evening and special occasions...wear stockings or pantyhose that glitter or are made of lace.

Thin legs can look scrawny in black or dark brown opaque...wear black sheers and skin tone shades instead.

And if you, and your legs, are feeling cute and coy...there are even tulle pantyhose to be had with ribbons and flowers at the ankles.

GET IN TOUCH WITH YOUR LEGS...TRY A LITTLE LEG WHIMSY...AND DRESS THEM TO LOOK THEIR BEST COMING AND GOING.

YOUR LEGS ARE POETS OF MOVEMENT...AND IT'S UP TO YOU TO DRESS THEM TO WIN A STARRING ROLE IN YOUR LIFE.

In tribal cultures, primitive men may have decorated and dressed their legs to please the Gods, but in modern times, it's up to a woman to decorate and dress her legs to please a man.

Health Tip...Support pantyhose is one of the most effective ways of preventing or relieving everyday tired, aching legs and minor varicosities...Support hosiery counteracts the effects of gravity by compressing the surface veins of the legs, which reduced the accumulation of blood in the veins.

knee know-how

Scrubs, rubs and beauty routines to revitalize knees

Give your legs a beauty break they deserve and crave.

Hot baths, too much sun, lack of exercise, rapid weight gain or loss can cause the skin on our legs to slacken. Neglected knees can become discolored and scruffy.

You can't shrug off the shape of your legs . . . but you can scrub off the texture of your knees. It takes knees, calves and ankles of silk to wear skirts of sizzling proportions.

Legs have fewer oil glands than other parts of the body, so they **need extra moisture** to stay smooth and supple.

When skin is dry, dead cells can collect on the surface, causing roughness. These dead cells collect beneath the surface, too, creating small, hard bumps that look like whiteheads.

leg scrubs and masks

Renourish the dull, dry skin on your legs with scrubs and masks that will banish bumps, smooth sandpaper knees, clear up spider veins, improve skin texture and elasticity, rev up circulation and smooth, soften, tone and tighten knees, calves and ankles.

1. While taking your bath or shower, gently scrub your legs from ankles to tops of thighs with a sloughing cream or loofah. Rinse, dry and slather on a rich body lotion.

2. Moisturize your legs with baby lotion to keep them glowing, massaging the fronts and backs of your knees as you cream them to improve the skin's texture and elasticity.

3. Massage lavish amounts of night cream into your legs to moisturize and renourish dry and flaky areas.

4. Use a fine-grain exfoliant on your knees. This will give them a sand-buffed effect as well as slough off deep layers of dead cells.

5. Tighten the pores on your knees and calves with a body-toning astringent like witch hazel (or any body-toning system from your favorite beauty counter).

6. Use a mask like one you would use on your face, to smooth and tighten slackened skin. Apply it from the knees down.

knee masks you can make at home

1. **Revitalize rough knees** with this fast-acting mask you make yourself. Mix one-half cup of table salt with enough lemon juice to make a paste. Wet knees, gently massage on the mixture and let it dry. Rinse it off in the shower, and cream your legs.

2. **Renourish your entire leg** with an avocado facial. Mash avocado and pack your legs with the paste. Leave on for 15 to 20 minutes, then rinse and towel dry.

3. **Deep moisturize kneecaps** with a simple hot-oil treatment just as you would your hair. Warm up a little olive oil and rub it into your knees. Apply plastic wrap to the area for ten minutes. Rinse off in shower and cream your legs.

the knee-and-calf massage

Kneading your knees and calves helps to prevent wrinkles, break down fat deposits, stretch and relax calf muscles and increase circulation.

Begin by smoothing on body lotion or leg reviver. Starting at the ankle, firmly knead the sides and back of leg with both hands. Work up to the top of the thigh. As legs absorb the moisturizing lotion, recream and massage with longer, stronger strokes.

Now apply moisturizing lotion to the kneecap and massage it with upward strokes. Beginning with the bottom fat pocket, work your way up to the top fat pocket, and then to the sides. When you feel heat rise under your fingers, you've stimulated circulation and are beginning to break down fat and cellulite.

---

back-of-the-knee massage

While seated, extend leg and rest heel on a chair in front of you. Massage lotion, in upward motions, from the top of the calf to the base of the thigh.

---

beauty tips

- Consider using a disposable shaver with a shaving gel while showering to remove unsightly hair from knees and legs.

- Hair-removing depilatories, waxes, or sanders are also available at a slightly higher cost.

- A revitalizing gel at the end of the day can rev up tired legs.

- Camouflage spider veins with a good waterproof cover-up cream.

- Night creams and day creams will keep your knees and calves polished and shining at all times.

- A firming lotion (or any astringent like witch hazel) after your bath or shower will stimulate the skin on your legs.

- Treat yourself to a professional massage whenever it fits into your budget. Swedish massage stimulates circulation and helps you relax.

- Break open a capsule of Vitamin E or primrose oil to help fade blue spider veins.

- Keep those feet pedicured. Pretty feet are a plus to great legs.

- Try to eliminate salt from your diet, since it can cause legs to swell.

- Drink eight glasses of water a day to flush out toxins in your system and prevent loss of elasticity in your skin.

- Don't sit with your legs crossed at the knee. The weight and pressure of one leg on the other can cut off circulation.

- Drink lots of orange, grapefruit and lemon juices. Vitamin C is essential for the production of collagen, a building block for a healthy epidermis.

knee-baring
How short is too short

Great legs can and should be flaunted at any age.

However, no-one wants to look ridiculous. So, if you're over 40, don't follow fashion's dictate to an extreme. Find a length that cuts your leg at its most flattering curve . . . anywhere from the middle of the knee to two or three inches above for starters.

Let the curve, tone and texture of your knees, calves and ankles guide you as to: how short is too short? rather than your age.

And as you work on your legs and see them improving, you can get more daring when your legs deserve more baring.

For evening . . . You can dare to bare more.

Wear the shortest skirts (full or straight) . . . with the highest heels . . . and the sheerest stockings.

For day . . . Take care and bare less.

No more than two or three inches above the knees and wear medium-high or flat shoes and boots. It's more appropriate, easier to maneuver and you'll feel less self-conscious.

Sit With Charm!

Walk With Grace!

Bend With Ease!

- Don't sit with your legs crossed. The weight and pressure of one leg on top of the other can cut off circulation.

- Sit with your legs crossed at the ankles, one behind the other so that the back of one ankle rests on the front of the other.

- Walk as if you were floating, with your shoulders back and your head held high. Don't bounce. Since gravity weakens our leg muscles, good posture is very important. Walking correctly strengthens and contours your legs.

- For modesty's sake bend from the knees —not the waist.

- Don't enter a car legs first. Instead, plant your legs on the ground and settle into the seat sideways. Turning forward, swing legs in.

knee language
Flirting with your knees

I've never met a man who wasn't a leg man! Have you?

Now that you've flexed, lifted, chiseled, rubbed, buffed and scrubbed your legs to perfection, they're ready to flirt.

Are yours: frivolous . . . flirtatious . . . flaunting?

If not, they can be!

Blushing Knees
Use a peach or tawny blush on your knees to highlight and contour much the same as you do on your cheekbones.

Scented Knees
Spray or dab your favorite scent on and behind your knees, calves and ankles. Legs should smell as irresistible as they look. Dab a few extra drops on a cotton ball, wrap in tissue and keep in purse for a sweet-smelling after-work pick-up.

Powdered Knees
Carry a small fluffy powder puff. Fluff your knees when you powder your nose. It's a sexy gesture that will turn an end-of-dinner yawn into an admiring grin.

Glittery Knees
For special occasions . . . or if you're just feeling out-right audacious . . . dust a little colored glitter on your knees so they sparkle and attract in the dark.

Winking Knees
Wear a pair of "winking eyes" Knee-cals™ on your knees. When you cross your legs, your knees will wink.

Sensational Legs

Invest in a pair of red high-heel pumps or close-toe sling-backs...wear them with black textured or sheer stockings. You'll turn every head when you enter a room.

Sassy Ankles

If you're just an old-fashioned girl at heart, why not wrap a yellow satin ribbon (or any other color) around your ankles, then tie it in a sassy bow!

If you would like a free pair of my winking eyes Knee-Cals,™ send a self-addressed, envelope, and $2.50 for shipping and handling (check or money order) to:
Babbie
331 W. 57th Street
Suite 133
New York, NY 10019

kneeing is believing
30 days later . . . the results!

30 DAYS LATER . . . It's back to Chapter One. Time to reknock your knees!

Remeasuring, comparing and rating the results of your efforts . . . making note of the bonus improvement in your posture, buttocks and thighs.

Now that you've followed Knockout Knees and Great Legs for 30 days,

You're ready to bare your knees . . .

Raise your hemline . . .

Kick up your sexier legs . . .

And dance the night away.

Since we've both accomplished what we set out to do, let's keep up the good work, and keep our legs looking their best for the next 20-plus years.

This book is small enough to fit into your purse, and important enough to pack into a suitcase.

Feeling great about the way you look is an attitude, not an age.

Didn't you just hear someone say, "You have knockout knees and great legs!"

	MON	TUES	WED	THURS	FRI	SAT	SUN
Posture improving practice							
Drinking 8 glasses of water							
Fencing and foiling around							
Swimming on dry land or in water							
Dancing with my feet							
Scissoring away at my flab							
Rubberband techniques							
Leg squeezes with my ball							
A variety of leg-er-cises at work, at home and at play							
Used my loofah to rev-up my circulation and exfoliate dead cells and scaley skin							
Gave my knees an oiling							
Soaked my feet in warm cream							
Exfoliated and annointed my entire legs with rich moisturizing creams							

About the Author

Babbie DeDerian is a published author, lecturer, spokeswoman and talk show guest. She is currently producing a new syndicated radio show to be called "Head-to-Toe BodyTalk."

She is also the author of *How to Have Beautiful Breasts at Any Age* (St. Martin's Press), which was serialized in *McCall's* and *Mademoiselle* magazines. She has lectured on the Cunard QE2, at the Learning Annex in New York City, and has conducted workshops around the country.

Ms. DeDerian is on the Advisory Board and a contributing writer for *Beauty Handbook*, a quarterly magazine. She also writes extensively for many other magazines and periodicals.